Alfred's Premier Piano Course

POP AND

Dennis Alexander • Gayle Kowalchyk • E. L. Lancaster • Victoria McArthur • Martha Mier

Alfred's *Premier Piano Course* Pop and Movie Hits Book 2B includes familiar pieces that reinforce concepts included in Lesson Book 2B. The music continues the strong pedagogical focus of the course while providing the enjoyment of playing familiar popular music.

The pieces in this book correlate page-by-page with the materials in Lesson Book 2B. They should be assigned according to the instructions in the upper right corner of each page of this book. They also may be assigned as review material at any time after the student has passed the designated Lesson Book page. Pop and Movie Hits 2B also can be used to supplement any beginning piano method.

Allowing students to study music they enjoy is highly motivating. Consequently, reading and rhythm skills often improve greatly when studying pop and movie music. The authors hope that the music in Pop and Movie Hits 2B brings hours of enjoyment.

Edited by Morton Manus

Produced by
Alfred Music Publishing Co., Inc.
P.O. Box 10003
Van Nuys, CA 91410-0003
alfred.com

Printed in USA.

ISBN-10: 0-7390-6690-0
ISBN-13: 978-0-7390-6690-4

CONTENTS

Use with Alfred's Premier Piano Course,
Lesson Book 2B, pages 4–5

Part of Your World
(from Walt Disney's *The Little Mermaid*)

Lyrics by Howard Ashman
Music by Alan Menken

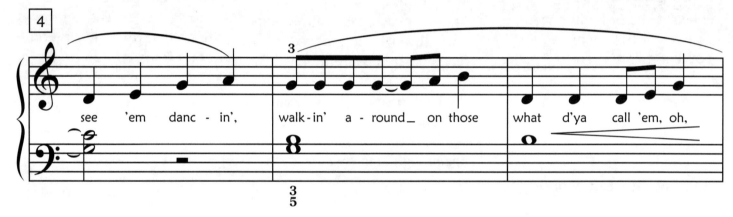

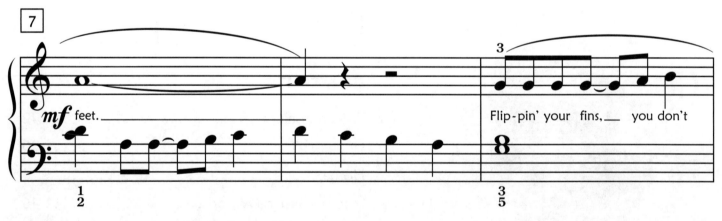

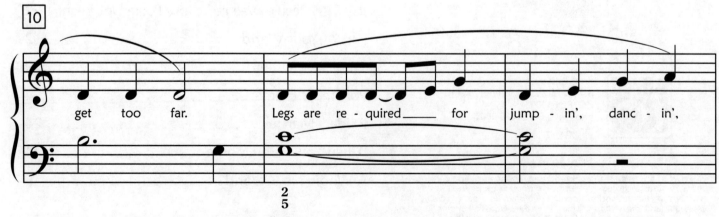

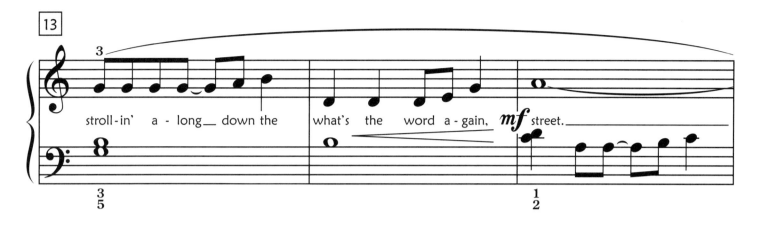

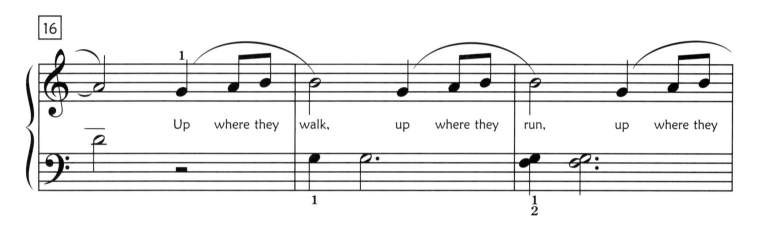

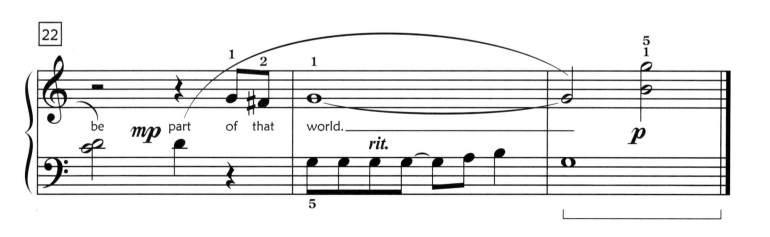

Pokémon (Theme)

Words and Music by
Tamara Loeffler and John Siegler

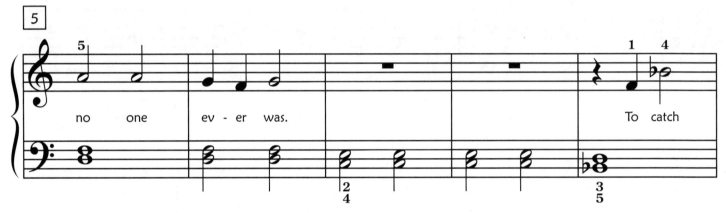

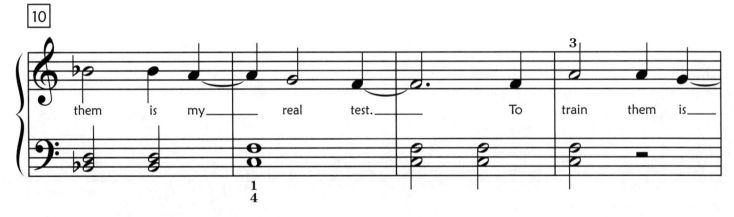

Home

Words and Music by
Michael Bublé, Alan Chang, and Amy Foster

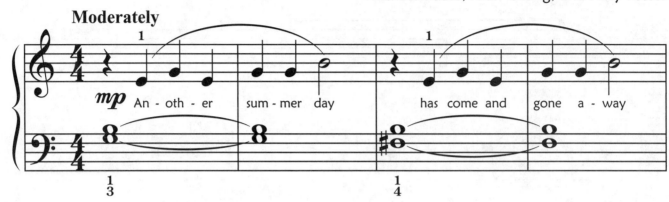

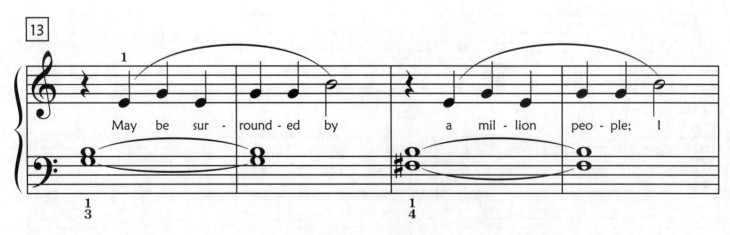

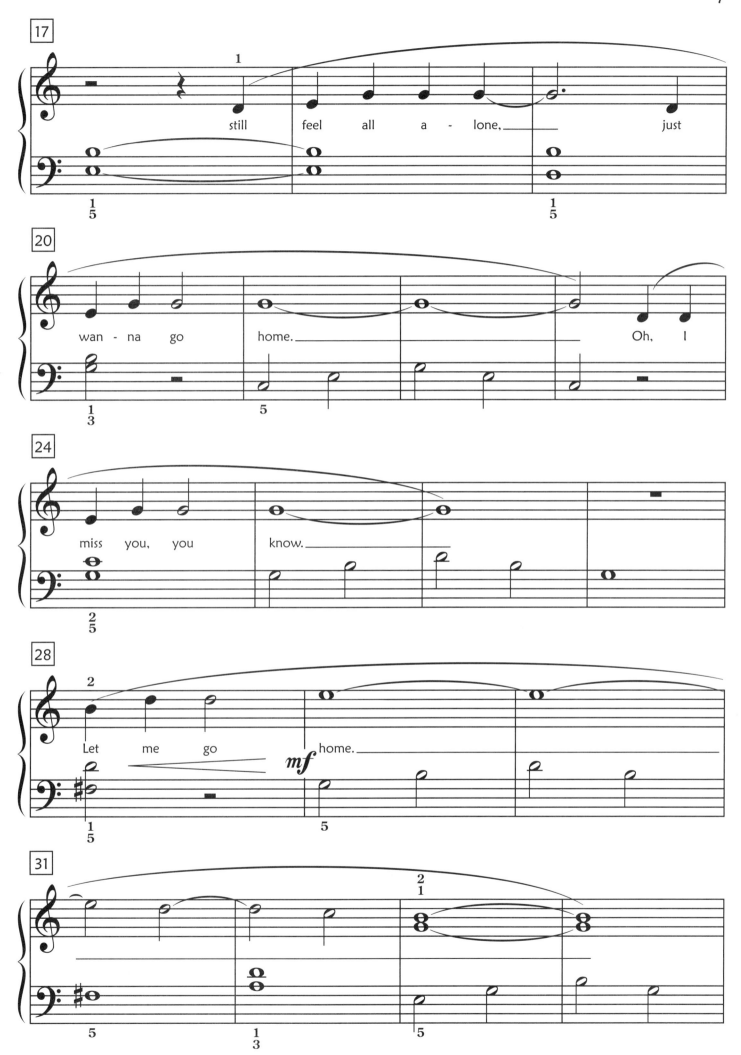

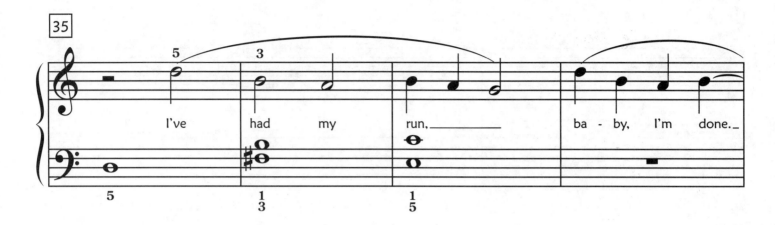

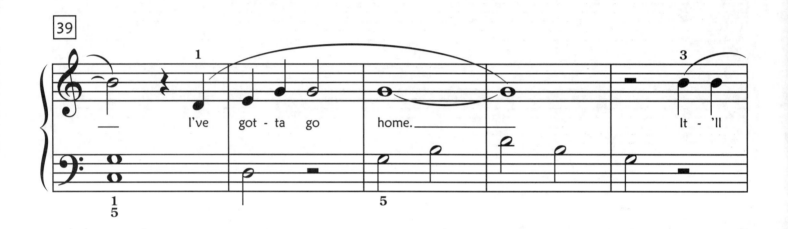

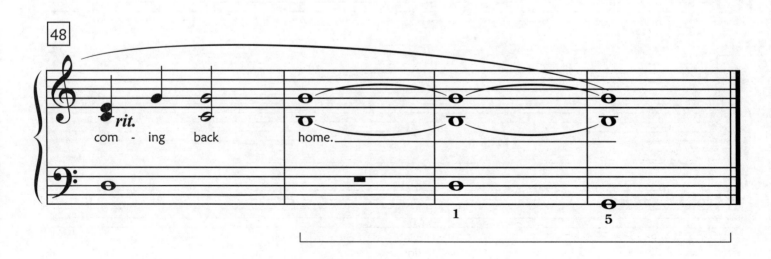

The Pink Panther

By Henry Mancini

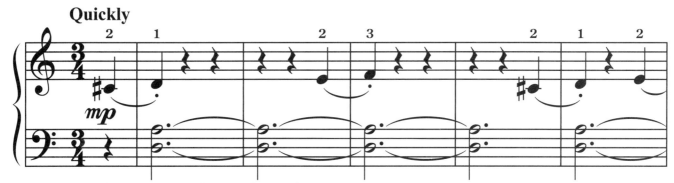

Both hands 8va lower throughout

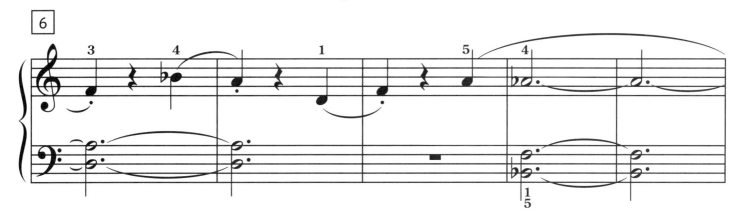

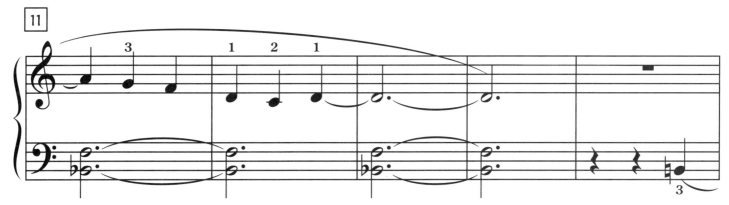

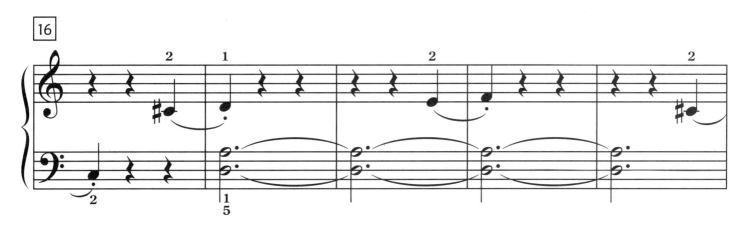

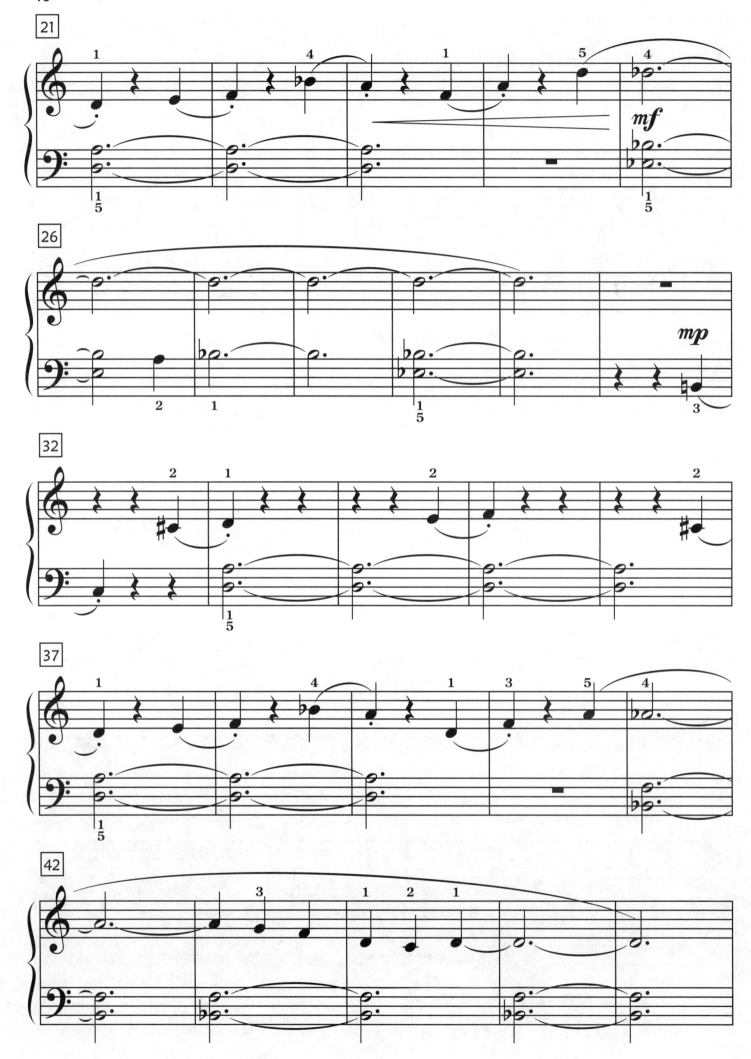

The Entertainer

Scott Joplin

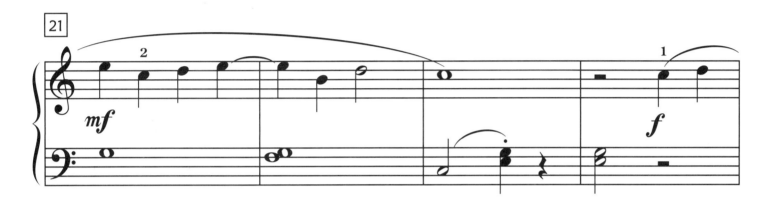

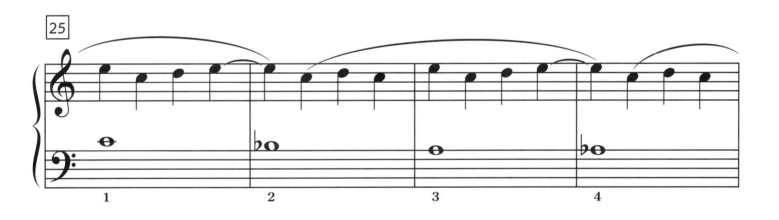

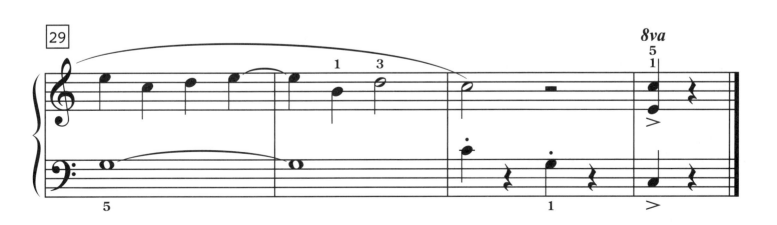

When You Wish Upon a Star

Words and Music by
Ned Washington and Leigh Harline

Moderately slow

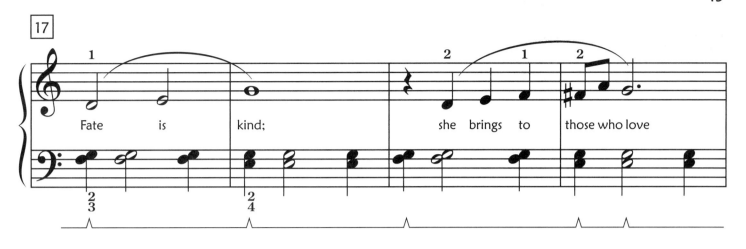

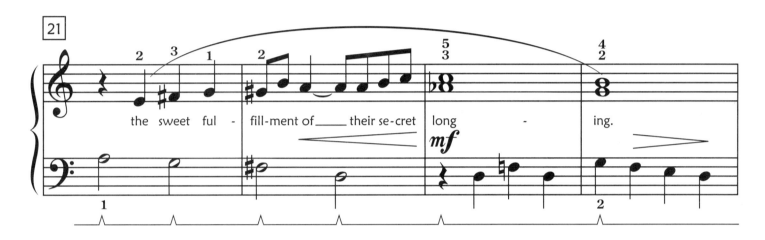

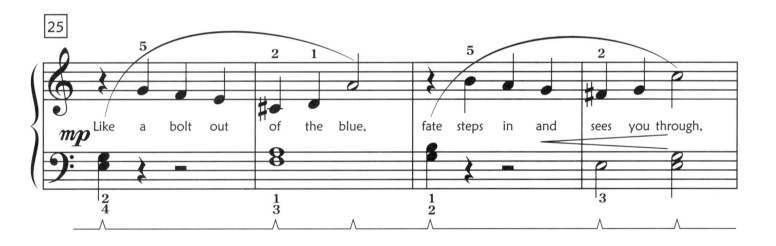

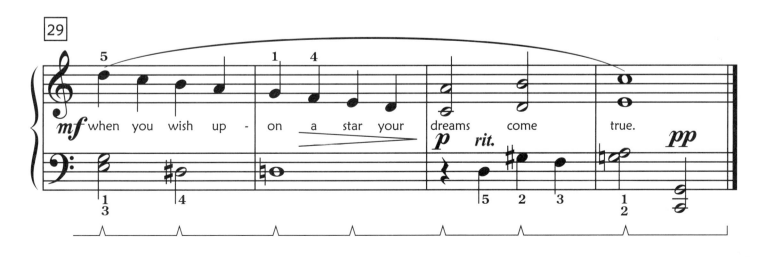

Hooray for Hollywood

Words by Johnny Mercer
Music by Richard A. Whiting

17

A Whole New World

(from Walt Disney's *Aladdin*)

Words by Tim Rice
Music by Alan Menken

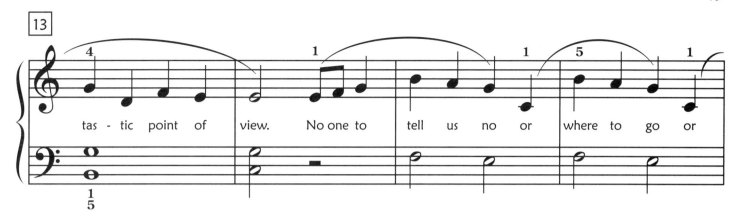

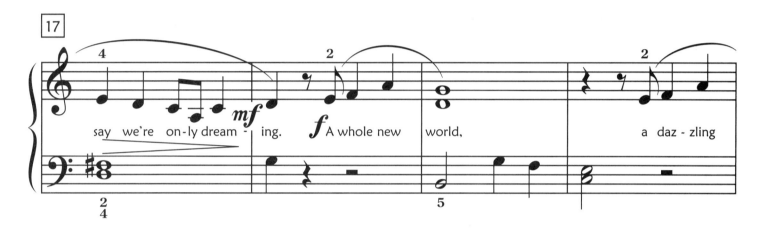

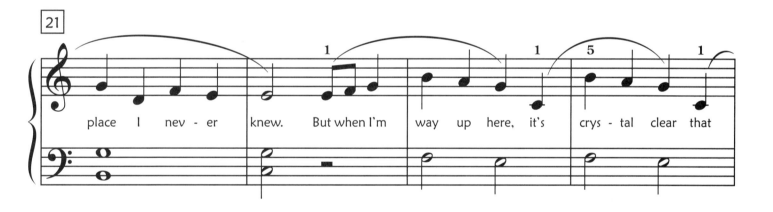

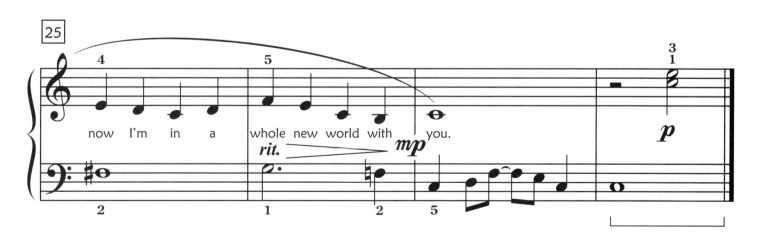

Hedwig's Theme

(from *Harry Potter and the Sorcerer's Stone*)

By **JOHN WILLIAMS**

Lesson Book: pages 44–45

Itsy Bitsy Teenie Weenie Yellow Polka Dot Bikini

Words and Music by
Paul J. Vance and Lee Pockriss

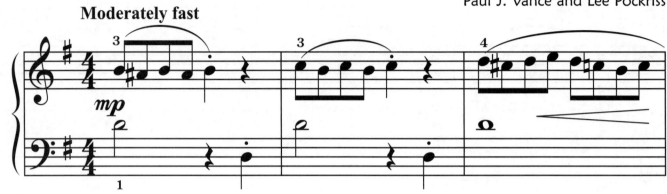

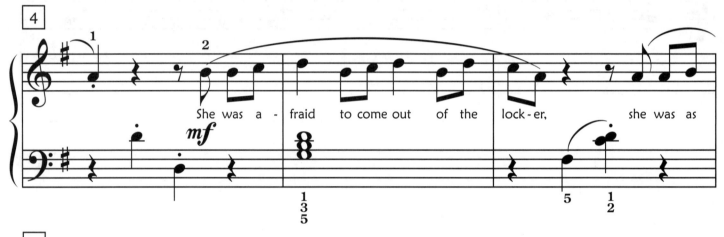

She was a-fraid to come out of the lock-er, she was as

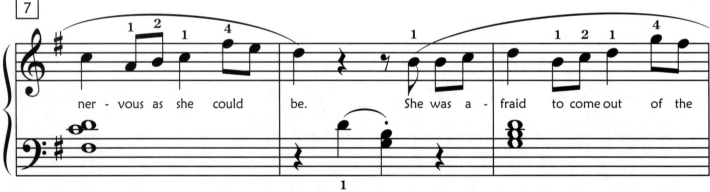

ner - vous as she could be. She was a - fraid to come out of the

lock-er, she was a-fraid that some-bod-y would see. (Two, three, four,

Lesson Book: pages 46–47

Raiders March

(from *Raiders of the Lost Ark*)

By **JOHN WILLIAMS**

Quick march tempo

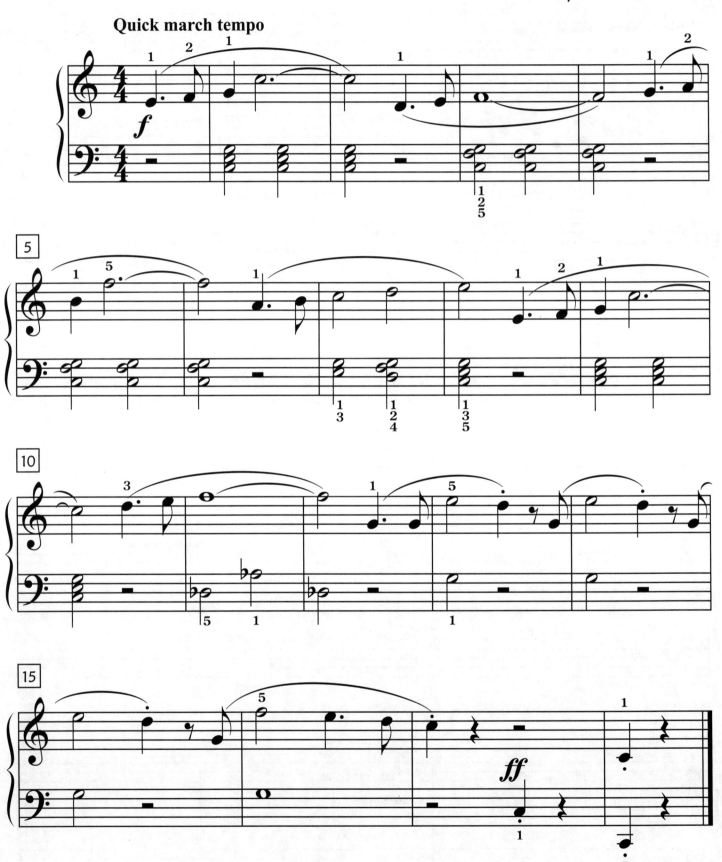